You Look So Good

(A Tribute to The Millions of Women, And the Million Men!)

Youssef Khalim

Copyright © 2012 Youssef Khalim

All rights reserved.

ISBN: 978-0-9787798-7-0
ISBN-13: 978-0978779870

DEDICATION

To: Larisa Khalim (The real or ideal soul-mate: inspiration).

       Tonya Tracy Khalim and

       Runako Soyini Khalim, (my most beloved daughters).

       Mother and Grandmother and Great-grandmother, (my most beloved maternal biological ancestors, and spiritual antecedents).

       M. A. Garvey (one of my 7 M's: my role models).

       Youssef Khalim II; III (my most beloved sons).

       Father and Grandfather and Great-grandfather, (my most beloved paternal biological ancestors, and spiritual antecedents).

To: The Forerunners and Reincarnation sources (beloved biological ancestors and spiritual antecedents), and

       The Almighty (our Spiritual Father), from whence we come.

CONTENTS

	Acknowledgments	i
1	Million Man March Prayer (Islamic Version)	1
2	Million Man March Prayer (Judeo-Christian Version)	Pg 2
3	Prayer	Pg 3
4	How Could You Not Know It?	Pg 4
5	Million Man March Blues	Pg 6
6	Let My People Go!	Pg 8
7	You Look So Good	Pg 10
8	Legendary Legs	Pg 13
9	Love Your Body	Pg 14
10	Attack The Jericho Wall!	Pg 15
11	A Man Will Do What A Man Must Do	Pg 16
12	Babylon, The Great, Bankrupt	Pg 17
13	Liberate Your Head	Pg 18
14	Headed For The Future	Pg 19
15	I Want To Thank You	Pg 20
16	We Orchestrate This Resurrection	Pg 21
17	Soldier's Prayer	Pg 23
18	Confession Time	Pg 24
19	Spirituals	Pg 25
20	Oasis of The Stars	Pg 26
21	Some Names Of God (In Prayer)	Pg 27

22	First, I Am	Pg 28
23	This World Is Mine	Pg 30
24	I Am That Jew, Just Like You	Pg 42
25	Declaration of The United People of The United States	Pg 47
26	She is The Temple of The Living God	Pg 58
27	Free At Last!	Pg 59
28	About the Author, And Other Books	Pg 61

ACKNOWLEDGMENTS

To: The Forerunners and Reincarnation sources (beloved biological ancestors and spiritual antecedents), and

The Almighty (our Spiritual Father), from whence we come.

1 MILLION MAN MARCH PRAYER
(Islamic Version)

In your name, Allah,
The Beneficent, the Merciful;
All praise to You, the Lord of the worlds;
The Beneficent, the Merciful,
Master of the Day of Judgment.

It is you that we serve.
It is from you that we ask for help.

Guide us on the right path,
The path of those upon whom You have bestowed favors,
Not those upon whom wrath is brought down upon,
Nor those who go astray.

Glorify Yourself in The Million Men, and
The 144,000, (and)
All those who choose
Freedom over tyranny,
Right over wrong,
And to be called Your Chosen,
In this Day of Judgment.

Show that those who are called
Babylon, the Great (or the Great Satan),
Are not great; but rather, those oppressors are low forms of life,
And will be put
Where they belong!

2. MILLION MAN MARCH PRAYER
(Judeo-Christian Version)

Our Father, Who is in Heaven,
Holy is Your Name.

Your Kingdom be strengthened
In the Million Men, and
The 144,000, (and)
All those who choose
Freedom over tyranny,
Right over wrong,
And to be called
Your Chosen,
In these Days of Judgment.

Show that those who are called
Babylon, the Great (or the Great Satan),
Are not great; but rather, those oppressors are low forms of life,
And will be put
Where they belong.

Give us this day
Our daily bread
And forgive us our debts,
As we forgive our debtors.

Lead us not into temptation,
But deliver us from all evil,

For Yours is the Kingdom
Of the Heavens
And the earth,
And the Power,
And the Glory,
Forever, and ever.

Amen.

3. PRAYER
(Judeo-Christian Version)

Our Father, Who is in Heaven,
Holy is Your Name.

Your Will be done to
Strengthen Your Kingdom
In Joshua, the earth, and Your Chosen,
As it is in Heaven.

Give us this day
Our daily bread
And forgive us our debts,
As we forgive our debtors.

Lead us not into temptation,
But deliver us from all evil,

For Yours is the Kingdom
Of the Heavens
And the earth,
And the Power,
And the Glory,
Forever, and ever.

Amen.

4. HOW COULD YOU NOT KNOW IT?

Why do lovers love to
Start their loving with a kiss?

When love adds on to perfect love
Does it create a list?

Each time we love completely,
Does time turn into bliss?

And if our love is meant to be,
How can we avoid it?

If a fire is set ablaze
Is a fire lit?

If the earth decides to turn
Can we make it quit?

If a chair is set aright
Does a chair sit?

If two hearts become one heart,
What happens if it splits?

If I am meant to be your lover,
How could you not know it?

When we pray to Our Father
Does water turn to mist?

If fate decides a matter
Can we choose to resist?

If Kingdom Come came here today,
Would it insist on staying,
Prayer, and praying,
Repentance,

Fasting,
Love, and
Saying: "The Kingdom of
Heaven's at Hand!

"For, lovers banded
Together;
Our love and Kingdom will last forever

"And love has triumphed because
I love you!
How could you not know it?"

5. MILLION MAN MARCH BLUES

You gave me your body
But you kept your mind and soul,

You gave me your body
But you kept your mind and soul.

You gave an empty shell
I need somebody whole.

You gave your word,
Then you went your way.

You went for night
'Cause I go for day.

You vote devils in
Though it is a sin
And yet, you say you are my friend.

You want to party
When I want to pray.

I move within the light
You want to worship might.

I choose a moral way,
You act like any snake.

You saw me heading south
So, you headed north.

You pulled the plug on me
As I was going forth.

You sent me cross the country
To make some history,

When, we all need
To be down on our knees.

I chose my words with care
Because they have some hope.

You need to watch your mouth
And wash it out with soap!

When I respect the earth,
You create urban blight.

And when I free the captive,
You say that *I'm* not right.

I gave you love
But you gave me shoes.

And sent me to March,
Gave me the Million Man Blues!

While I was aiding elders,
You deserted my child.
Baby, you should stay away awhile.

You gave me your body
But kept your mind and soul,

You gave me your body
But kept your mind and soul.

You gave an empty shell
I need somebody whole!

6. LET MY PEOPLE GO!

Gather together in Unity
Those of you who love Me,
Go down to D.C.

Tell Pharaoh
To let My People Go!

Get up, and form a Million Strong
Camp-out around the Capitol Dome
Say to My Chosen: "Come back home!"

Believe with all your heart and soul.
Stand tall,
And Babylon, the Great, will fall!

Get up, my people, march!
And choose to play the leading part.

Tell Pharaoh:
"The time has come,
Your time is up,
Your cup is full of iniquity
And you are history, you demon!

You are driven from the earth as
You were driven out of heaven!

The time is really late,
And freedom can no longer wait!
And, God has sent some men to tell you:

I want the earth back,
It is time for you to pack,

Hide from my wrath,
And watch your mouth!

The rejected is
The cornerstone of This House!"

Get up, Mighty Million Strong!
You are by no means alone.
Go down to D.C.!

Where Malcolm, Marcus, Martin, Mohandas, Moses,
Muhammad camp out.

And no man can number the unseen Armies
That drive the devils from power!

At last, My Chosen are coming home:
The ones who choose right over wrong.

Pharaoh will surely let you go:
For he will be
Deposed!

7. YOU LOOK SO GOOD

You look so good
I want to give you
All my money,
All the honey, and the sweetness we can find.

I want to give you
All my love
Anything you want,

And all the sunshine
Anytime you want some light.

You make my day!
Anytime I think of you
And when I see you, everything is right!

What a sparkle!
You should get a patent for your loveliness,

The prize for gracious, gorgeous-
Wow! I feel good just thinking about you,
Because you look so good!

You look radiant, and wonderful,
Just like summer is flower filled.

I'd love to know you,
Have you,
Any day,
To make my day,
Forever,
And compensate for all my former lifetimes
Before I met you,
Because you look so good!

But, it's not just money I want to give.

For, to give to you is to truly live!
And believe me, you make me come alive! And see:

You look so good,
I want to invite you out to dinner,
With our Father (He rules the universe),
So we can sit and chat awhile!

You look so good that
I'll think of you on every day,
And find a way to please you every minute!

You look so good,
You may not be for real!

You look so good,
I just want to reach out and touch you!

You look so good,
I just want to inhale
The warmth that surrounds you!

You look so good that
Even though I just met you today,
I want to love you yesterday!

You look so good
I want to take you home,
"Turn you every which way but loose,"
And give you everything you ever
Thought you wanted,
And love you forevermore!

And, you look so good,
I just want to thank you for being born!

So, it's not just money I want to give
For, to give to you is to truly live!
Believe me, you make me come alive!
And see:

All your honey,
And your sweetness
And I love you,
Sweetly... for it.

Thank God for eyes
To look at you
"He" must be proud of how you look!

For, beautiful has triumphed,
Just as surely as will truth!

And we know just by seeing you:
In the end,
We will win!

Because you make me so alive, to see
That "Truth and Beauty" always wins,
Because it is so good!

8. LEGENDARY LEGS

I love every inch
Of your gilded body
And legendary legs:

I love your
Mouth and mind,
Eyes and vision,
Thoughts and feelings-
Until
The deserts transform themselves into vast wetlands,
Thriving with trees,
And bursting forth with flowers,

And until
I've loved every single inch
And imagination
Of your gilded, beautiful body
And Long Legendary Legs!

9. LOVE YOUR BODY

Yes, I still love
To see your eyes,
And I still want to love
Your body.

But I also want to love
You throughout
Your mind and soul,

Until I can listen
To what your mind says
 With or without spoken words.

And our souls
Become one joyous,
Sparkling, spark of light,
Radiating brilliantly, while Heaven rejoices:
Because I've loved
Every infinite trace of you!

And you feel loved
In every infinitesimal trace of
You.

10. AND NOW, ATTACK THE JERICHO WALL!

African man, standing tall,
Thanks for coming to the mall

I do truly love you all;
You look so good there, wall to wall!

Now, you have heard the final call,
And I hereby anoint you all

I am giving you the ball,
Attack the Jericho Wall!

11. A MAN WILL DO WHAT A MAN MUST DO

A man will do
What a man must do,
And you cannot keep him down!

You can't stop a man with his mind made up
Or walk in front of a speeding truck,
And live to make a fuss!

A man will try to reason with you;
He'll try to tell you what is true.

If you oppress, and treat him wrong
You'll get a war before too long!

A man will fight you day and night!
A man believes that right makes might!

A man will rise, resist, rebel!
A man will send you- straight to hell!

12. BABYLON, THE GREAT, IS BANKRUPT

I once was lost
But now, I'm found.
I stand on higher ground.

It seemed so late
And Babylon, the Great
Was strong, wrong, wide, and long.

But, then you came along.

You made that Babylon, the Great, bankrupt!
And then, You said,

"Get up, My People, the time is late!
That oppressor snake is dead!
It's time for you to move ahead.

"So, bury Babylon
Don't take too long!

"Then move to higher ground."

13. LIBERATE YOUR HEAD

Ok. If you want to be free
Come on, you Chosen, listen to Me!

But if you want to wander another 40 years
Then, keep on closing up your ears!

Now, I only want for you to see,
You are made in the image of Me!

So, repent, atone, and come to Me
And, you will see Me set you free!

Cooperate, and care, and share, And there will be
no devils there!

And, when you end your selfish ways
Your nights will turn to lovely days.

Include My Will in all your life
For, you must be part of the Christ!

Now, watch your mouth, choose your words with care,
And you'll create a Heaven there!

Fill your life with love, and faith and trust,
And I will surely lift you up!

And, if you worship Me in truth,
Pharaoh will surely turn you loose!

But, you must apply what your prophets said,
And it will free you, mind & body-
And liberate your head!

14. HEADED FOR THE FUTURE

Headed for the future
Headed for the sky

They are going to love me
And, I'll tell you why:

GOD IS GREAT! GOD IS GREAT!
GOD IS GREAT! GOD IS GREAT!

And I'll tell you why...

Because, we're headed for the future
Headed for the sky

They are going to love me
And I'll tell you why

God is Great, (it's evident!)
God is Great, (it's evident!)
God is Great, (it's evident!)

And I'll tell you why.

15. I WANT TO THANK YOU

I want to thank You, (Father),
For all you've done for me.

I want to thank you,
Because you set me free!

I want to thank You,
Because you let me see.

I want to thank You, (Father),
You give true liberty!

16. WE ORCHESTRATE THIS RESURRECTION

In Your name, Allah: The Beneficent, The Merciful
All Praise to You, Allah, the Lord of all the worlds.

You are the Orchestrator over all things
And gave free will to human beings.

So we can learn to choose, and grow
And life returns to You and knows

That You are the Magnificent One
Your Golden Age is at its dawn.

And as it did so long ago
Your stellar light will wax and glow.

You string the galaxies with a finger
Waved across the sky,
And turn Black Holes into illuminating
Thoughts that never die.

You throw, and then can catch the light
And all you ever made was truly a delight.

You fathom where the darkness hides
With man your patience has abided.

You braid "The laws of nature"
Into long and flowing locks
Man is the key, using his head;
In time, you are the clock.

You close life up in a tiny seed
That grows and dies, then lives and feeds.

And long ago my fathers said,
"Surely, our Lord can raise the dead."

You made the green a color; & blue the gate beyond
In this, the Resurrection, the good are coming home.

You freeze-up fire, decree the fall of snow
You ration wind, & make it swirl and blow;

You hold the rain in your loving cup
Love's endless use won't use You up;

You slice up time, place us in space
When we forgive, you give us grace;

You warm our heart when we feel ill,
Created cold so we can chill;

You are truly the Inscrutable One
& know all things before they're born;

You guide creation, the flocks and herds.
(Oppressors will get what they deserve!)

Moses, Muhammad, and Jeshua are the guiding ones
And all mankind is Allah's son.

You give Christ-links to guide our way,
That spirit is here with us today

To orchestrate the promised land, and
Redeem the just with a Mighty Hand!

17. SOLDIER'S PRAYER

Our Lord & Master of the Universe,
We sing of You in praise & verse

You intervene at our request
And grant us only what is best.

You give us chances to enhance & build
And show us how to choose, & develop skill.

You teach us about honor & the truth
And help us safeguard our precious youth.

You teach us Unity & trust in you
To have faith in You is the right thing to do!

You help us clearly see deniers & oppressors,
As You retake the earth from the liars & detractors.

Forgive our sins we have committed,
Forgive the things we have omitted.

Let us be the soldiers to make your Kingdom sure
To uproot the evil ones, you are the cure!

We submit to you, the Almighty & All-Seeing,
And work to bring your world into being.

18. CONFESSION TIME

I confess that:

God is Great!
God is Great!
God is Great!

I confess, there is no God, but God!
I confess, there is no God, but God!
I confess, there is no God, but God!

I confess, Moses is His Messenger.
I confess, Jeshua is His messenger.

I confess, The Carmelites are His!

I Confess, there is no God , but God!

For all time,

I confess that

God is Great!

19. SPIRITUALS
(This is what Yoga does.)

The soothing mist comes pouring through
The right sphere of my mind.

Then, cooling current flows into my heart
And up and down the gateway to my soul.

It makes a subtle shroud about my chest & shoulders,
Fills the left side of my mind,

And forms a force field to the bottom of my spine.

It swells & forms a bulbous aura around my being;

And I submit.

Then, I am One with all the Universal One;

And I am whole.

At resonance, I think a Holy thought
To add the force to carry on.

Your Holy Spirit visits make Your Kingdom firm.

20. OASIS OF THE STARS

It's time to bring the Kingdom into being,
Make the Word our warm companion,
Bless the good with brotherhood
From sea to shining sea,

The heart forgives, & Justice forms another
Heartbeat always in the minds of men,

That we become the Light & share the gifts of God,
And earth is the oasis of the stars,

That work becomes a joy we welcome,
Joy becomes an ornament we wear
As we establish goodness.

And we make music wings that lift to lofty planes,
With roots that water from the sources of the soul.

That everyone is judged from
Record Books that show their path through time,

The evil ones reveal themselves by pushing at
His Winds of Change. The Lord will
Put the evil ones in chains!
And all God's chosen work to bring His Kingdom into being.

21. SOME NAMES OF GOD (IN PRAYER)

You provided Safety to me
You turned what seemed adverse into a Blessing
You lead to Understanding.

You put a shield around my family,
Adopted them,
And You protect their steps.

You give Great Love
And let me see your Mercy,
Teach me in your ways.

You lift me with your Kindness, touch my heart.
And You are Glorious, Supreme,
The Originator of All Things.

I wish to stay within your Grace,
Embrace your Light,
And be of those submitting ones;

And bring good families into You, to Safety,
To Benefit from your Warm Heart (& Names),
Then name the World as You, Yourself, Allah,

Sees

Fit.

22. FIRST, I AM

First, was I. And I am Glorious, Magnificent, Infinite, Supreme; for, I am God.

    I'm in the solar winds that come to earth to sustain it, for, I am He who sustains and shares. For instance, you can see me as the Aurora Borealis, or the southern lights as I enter through the magnetic poles. However, I permeate the earth much more subtly with my energies and with my forces; and I create whatever exists on earth. In fact, I am the source behind all suns and planets, and behind whatever exists. I give and I share and I take and I bestow.

    I am One. I am the Creator of all things. You, my children, are created in my image and you are polarized and magnetic like my earth. When I come into you, I enter much like I do through all my creation: primarily through the north node, and you feel this as ecstasy, joy, or insight. Therefore, I am the breath of life. And I am knowledge.

    Some of you can see me enter you (in visions) as Light, much like the Aurora Borealis. I AM THE LIGHT, coming from near and distant places, and looking down onto the earth; and looking out onto my galaxies.

    I look out or in, to or from my most finite or august creations, and when I fill you with light, you too can look out or in, like me, but this is on a scale appropriate to you. For, I am ever moderate to you, and I do not overload you, to blow a fuse, when you submit.

Today, you are given a choice of turning toward me, or perishing, through a story about my Oneness, and of my love, and of my sharing nature. Everything is mine, and I am today bringing many changes to the earth, and you must live in my ways to even survive on the earth plane. FOR THE TIME IS AT HAND!

The recent Desert Storm War was an example of the continuing struggle of the haves against the have-nots; and it was about oil, greed, power, and selfishness. It was a major event setting into motion many changes of nations, peoples, and relationships. Economies based on war industries and aggression, and the various evils will be cut off. The necessities and amenities, and their distribution can be available when the will is present. The old economics is dead! Society must be restructured! The oppressions must cease! It is time you know about me and know that :

    THIS WORLD IS MINE!

23. THIS WORLD IS MINE

Make no mistake
The time is late
I'm taking my world back from devils
Lining them up for hell
And giving to my chosen
What they earn.

And forever more, I will be good to those who are good.

For, I am love, I am light
I am He, look to me

I am reconciliation
Recover, in me, I am first causation

I am judgment, differentiation
I weigh person-by-person, and nation-by-nation

I am forgiveness, merciful and kindly
I am healing the memories, I am moving, and mindful

I am everywhere, and in all things
I see all the worlds in the mist of my being

I am Glorious, sublime, I am Great
I made you, And I know (what I make)

I am fearless, and peerless; I am seer
I am healing the ailing, I am the miracle maker

I am caring, and sharing; And I am dashing
I am paring the devils for a thorough thrashing
I am Lord of lords, & justice is mine,
I separate the good from the other kind

For, I am love, I am Light
I am He, look to me

Make no mistake
The time is late
I'm taking my world back from devils
Lining them up for hell
And giving to my chosen
What they earn

For, first was I
Then, I made you (like me)
For, I can do whatever (choices),
And, I choose

And some of you choose me
And choose to be with me, like me; Love Me
(I love you too)
I truly love you too:
You are My Chosen

Anyway, after I made you, I became you, also.
For, you move and have your being in me.

But some of you rebelled and became (and still are) devils because you try to distance yourself from Me, and you choose evil.

I let the devils rule my earth, (in their last major time of rule), since about the time of the Renaissance. So, the Western world, especially, became a kind of "new" Rome, or Greece.

The good things you see are mostly the work of my chosen and Me. (And you should remember that I can bring good out of what is bad).

The values, outlook, and institutions of those who rule, bring ruin and deprivation to my earth. They are essentially materialists, and they esteem, even worship things: cars, houses, clothes, jewelry, animals, people, gadgets.

In fact, devils would rather worship anything but Me, their ONE and ONLY Maker. And they go to war over what they esteem, or worship, which are things and gadgets- not principles. This is another way that they prove they are devils.

They also go to war because they have a very irrational, and destructive economic and social order. And they are generally involved in efforts to preserve, protect, or advance it. So, that war was also used to advance the interests of one of their allies, the State of Israel. But those who promote that order show that they are devils, especially when light has come to them showing its true nature. And the devils also go to war in acts of ego gratification, selfishness, greed, and oppression. Devils like to oppress people.

Anyway, their distance from Me helps create their faulty, narrow, and defective perceptions and judgments.

But remember, all of you are at different levels of development because of your different experiences, and because of your individual efforts throughout your evolutionary journey. Remember, distance from Me will create defects in your mind, body, and soul.

So, come in close
Stay close to me, for I am He
Who made you.

I am you, self; I am He
What you do to the least of them, you do to me

Like an ideal brother, I am your friend
As your Father, I am your kin

I am African, Native American, European, and more
I am all mankind in One, I am top-drawer

I am Jew, Hindu, Muslim, Christian, and more than these.
I am One, man is one; I see deeds, not creeds

It is written: "the earth is the Lord's which you can see
I'm not kidding, I'm taking it back for me

I watched as the 7th World Empire formed itself into the 8th Power arrangement. And by seeing this, my chosen must realize THE TIME IS AT HAND!

And they gathered themselves together in the plains of Meggido (for war).

But remember, my children, the battle of Armageddon is simply the war of the haves against the have-nots. And this has, and is occurring all over the world- in Asia, in Europe, in Africa, in America. And devils will use the UN or any other vehicle to do their deeds. AND I, GOD, WILL SURELY WIN THE WAR AGAINST THE OPPRESSORS!

IN FACT, YOU OPPRESSORS CAN SLASH THE PRICE OF OIL TO ROCK BOTTOM PRICES (WHILE EVERYTHING ELSE DOUBLES OR TRIPLES IN PRICE) BUT YOU WILL STILL GO BANKRUPT, BECAUSE YOU ARE A DEAD SNAKE. AND IT IS TIME FOR YOU TO GO TO HELL!

Now, just watch, as I confound the devils. For I can make you lose when you win. And I can make you win when you lose. You must be sure that what you do is right and just. And you cannot justify what is unjust by invoking Christianity, or Islam.

For, I gave Jesus, Muhammad, I give you the Lights
And you gave me the lie, you put might over right

I see your "new world order," it's more of the same:
Controlling oil price, protecting Zionists is the Old World game

My chosen choose to be like me, and not like the devil
Do you see me reflected in the colony state called Israel?

My "Jews" are the righteous individual(s) nations, and the just
They'll inherit the world, and in me they trust

I saw you hijack the UN, you great deceiver
I gave you a free hand to show how deep rooted is your evil

I saw rich get rich to filthy, you take more than you need
I saw you slaughter my people, every dastardly deed

I weigh the heart and the deeds; I have found you wanting
You lie-cheat, kill-steal, destroy: the mark of Satan

You co-opt the free will on my very own children
You are shameless devils, you are not Christian

You make endless have-nots, you forgot about Me
I'm taking my world back, 'Cause I am the key

I am the Word, I am the One
I am the Way, I'm watching you!

Make no mistake, I'm watching you:

You are the loud mouth defective devils
Your time is up for getting it together

You have been here many times before
You are still evil like long, long ago

You don't treat others like you want to be treated
You are conceited; and you will be unseated
You glorify your bombs and guns, you are children of Cain
You love to kill, don't you? Something's wrong
With your brain!

   Now, for those pseudo-Christian and pseudo-Muslims who fear to take up their cross and follow Me because they love ease and "the good life." They are really decadent, and degenerate, and defective in their souls, and they give lip service to the tradition of Abraham. And they support, and only want to fit in to the existing evil, satanic economic and social order. And they are fellow travelers with the devil.

You fear the cross because you
Are a bloodthirsty devil and liar
You are the opposite of Jesus,
And fit for the fire

Choose well, Remember Moses
Opportunity knocks; the window closes

   George Bush was the president of the US, and the visible leader of the war effort. His efforts highlighted the fact that the 8th Power Arrangement was forming. Contrast how he behaved in Desert Storm (or toward Panama) and how he behaved toward Israel. Also notice how Israel treated him.

You occupy Panama to stamp out corruption and drugs
In your failure, reflect on your homegrown thugs

Now if King George can overthrow and install governments at
His whim
PRC could overthrow him (& his court of lackeys & wimps)

Big, bad King George Bully is a mighty warrior
(Against the weak and poor)
When opposed by Israel, he turns wimpy
(Routinely, they show him the door)

If it takes a big strong man to pulverize his weak brother
Let me see you go beat up your mother

Israelis deserve love and security like anybody else
Everybody must be treated equally, no more, no less

The righteous are sometimes targeted by the devil
And that cause of war is evil

I repeat: If you don't want it done to you
Don't do it to them or him; this is truth

Make no mistake, the time is late: I'll bless my good with brotherhood
And rid the earth of some; and rid the earth of scum

Now, here is the sum of my timely song
Devils don't know the difference between right and wrong

(Devils don't know the difference between right and wrong!)

So, the devils may try to kill some of you
They show that they are devils; that's what devils do

Don't fear them; have love, and faith, and trust
The good I gather into me, and dust returns to dust

But, if they threaten you with their guns
At judgment time, I'll burn their buns

And if you don't want to "burn," learn to share. Leadership in the new age (which is upon us) will be in sharing and caring. It's easy. Just be like Jesus. Be like Moses and Muhammad, and Noah. Be like Me, because I made you like that.

I share wealth, skills, knowledge, and time
I am the One Creator, the universe is mine

I am love, I am law
I am leaving to where you are

For I am God with you, I am God with us
I am the One and Only God to trust!

And remember, if you think Jesus will protect,
Shield, or intercede for you
Go back and check out how
And who Jesus prayed to

Open your eyes, my children. And realize how the evil economic and social order works (at home and abroad). AND KNOW THAT I, GOD, AM ENDING IT NOW, IN THESE TIMES. Reflect on the various military and other actions taken by leaders of that failed order.

The traitors and the evil ones bring on the "Voodoo Economics" and then of necessity
Need Gunboat diplomacy to enforce it.
My patriots will displace
The devils inch by inch

The evil ones follow Script closely and embargo
Freeze assets, redline, blacklist, blockade, blackball
(From their Whitehouse)
All who won't join their evil cabal

John foretold of 666:
Good and ultra-bad don't mix

Now the 7th Power are these: USA UK Canada Australia
I am the Infinite Power and undefeatable

AND I WILL END THE 7TH POWER, AND I WILL END THE 8TH POWER BECAUSE MY POWER IS EVERLASTING.. And I Am omniscient. I see what you do:

You levy too much on the elders and poor
You are like ravenous wolves gnawing at the door

Some of your CEO's get 110 times the average worker
You reflect corrupt communists, maybe a little dirtier

You allowed enough liberty
To unleash the creative genius of my children
You use their creations to enslave them,
You are no good, Satan

You encourage some to be foulmouthed,
Disrespectful clowns, and to act like monkeys
I am Divine, and gave each some
And you must be like Me

John called the 7th Power the
"Great Satan," which is true
Come out of her my people,
For I have come for you

Make no mistake
The time is late

For, first, was I. For, I Am God.
And yes, I'm in the winds, the rain, the plains,
The sun, the moon
(*The* Judgment Day is coming soon)

I am in the breath you breathe
I'm in your walk
You open your mouth, I'm in your talk

I'm in your car where Body is Make
I even reside in "Shake And Bake"

I channel the Mississippi flow
I make it all good: for those who know

I'm in the earth, the trees, and seas

And bees know Me, and know their place
For, *everything moves and has its being in me*

Make no mistake
The time is very, very late
And he who hesitates exceeds the limits
Because I'm taking back my world from devils
Lining them up for hell
And giving to my chosen
What they earn.

And forever more, I will be good
To those who walk with Me

WE'LL WALK *TOGETHER* ON MY EARTH
And sing my song
And know the difference between right and wrong
Move in my will
And share the knowledge and the skills

AND YOU WILL KNOW THAT I AM LOVE
For, I will bathe you in my light
I will lift you with my might
You will *see* that I'm ALL RIGHT

You will see that I am He
For, you will *look* at me

FOR, FIRST AM I. FOR, I *AM* GOD

It's time
You know Me.
Know it!
Show It!

THIS WORLD IS MINE!

24. I AM THAT JEW, JUST LIKE YOU

I am that Jacob Jew, like you
My soul is shaken, grief wells up like high tide
Though I had four wives, My true love,
Rachel's gone; Sun, Joseph disappeared
My right hand, Benjamin is captive
My heart is somber; they need to number 12.

I am that Solomon,
And looked for Rachel 'mongst a thousand wives
(Still was not satisfied); so I wrote books,
Fathered the world through Jewish blood,
Collected horses, built The Temple
Minted gold, tried to gather wisdom
Lost our Kingdom
(The sons I got were wanting),
Rachel was not there.

Thomas Jefferson is my name
I am the 3rd King of the realm.
In image, I am Solomon & Jacob: Rachel's gone
I am in line to seize the throne.
In life, do right; take time to pray
(My Twin & I died the very same day).

I am that John, the son of Zebedee,
& Jew par excellence
Here's how to get the radiance:
Submit as Jesus did."

I am that Stevie Wonder Jew
(Rachel & I are a song for two)
And sing of love, redemption, justice
Righteousness, and truth.
On any given day, I just think to say,
"I love you."

I am the princess Jews:
Like Ruth, & Ester, sister, Mary, Naomi, aunts, Sacagawea, wives, Joan of Arc, Elizabeth, Sojourner Truth, Gwendolyn; our mothers (& their line of Queens).

I am the Jews who fight oppression, fight for knowledge, light, and right, like: Isaac Newton, John Milton, Yasser Arafat, Lyndon Johnson, John Brown, Nat Turner, Frederick Douglas, Mahatma Gandhi, Kwame Nkrumah, Julius Nyrere, Chief Joseph, Marcus Garvey, King James (who published the Holy Book), W.E.B. Dubois, Sigmund Freud, Malcolm X, Martin Luther King Jr., Albert Einstein, Johann Kepler, Gamel Nasser, Ras Tafari, Mozart, George Washington Carver, Cyrus (the Persian), Omar Khayyam, Confucius, Rabbi Judah Hanasi, Harold, (and other Washingtons) numberless others; Miles Davis, John Coltrane (all my children are the same).

But when will Rachel come?

I am that Muslim Jew, Muhammad,
I am the Messenger of God
I am That Other Prophet, like the Sun
I am the likeness of that Moses Jew,
And give the law:
The 3 religions of the West are One, born of Abraham.
And there is One religion of the West, in 3.
As, there is One mankind in 5 races,
One Islam in 5 pillars;
One God, viewed from the Third planet, in 3 aspects,
Who gave no sons because Rachel was not there.

(Black) John, the Baptist,
I am the Jew called Jean Baptiste DuSable,
I pitched my tent where crossroads of the universe diverge;
Was set to become a rabble-rouser
But Rachel was not there, so
I died in 1818, was born again that year as Charles Marx, the Jew who fashioned "isms" Strong enough to shake foundations, & the systems,
Hold at bay the devil
'Til I came to term.

I am that Abraham Lincoln, Jew
I have come back to speak with you.
What I said then is always true.
When right makes might, that will see you through.
Mary & I... (will see you through).

I am Abraham,
The father of the Jews.
The Gospel, news is that Jews
Follow truth and justice; righteousness.
Jews follow Christ, and not the anti-Christ (OPPRESSORS).
I confess, OPPRESSORS ARE THE DEVILS!
You know my children (by the way
They choose).

I am King David, Jew
The Queen and I have a Kingdom to rule;
Bathsheba was a very special prize
But married to a homosexual, Uriah
(As it was said).
He fought within our army cadres.
Forgive the trust I have betrayed
By offing him.
(Without delay, the current King)

Will put Uriah back into the Army again)
Showing that we all get many chances:

God gave me mercy and a son
The Lord, He gave us Solomon
& I proclaim, my Lord is One
His arm is Christ, the Son.

Some Druze are Jew; Baha'is too; some Sikhs; some Zoroastrians, Hindus, Buddhists,
Muslims, Socialists, Adventists, Mormons, "Witnesses."
Some "Jews" are even Jews
(For a Jew is: love of God and of one's fellow man; justice, liberty,
Freedom, knowledge, LIFE).

I am that Jesse Jackson Jew (for God exists).
I am the image of the liberating King (for evils we resist),
Was put aside because this latest king must be elected.
King George (Saul), must be defeated.
So, Vernon Jordan baptized him in living colors,
Anointed him beside none other than the Potomac.
We must rise up against the wicked,
Then, see if Rachel comes.

I am that Jew in concentration camps, (or "Egypt").
I learn to TRUST IN GOD, not things, for He surrounds us.

And know, we all are Jews. All Jews, always connected!
All people (are connected) just like
Jacob & Rachel throughout infinity,
So, all my sons and daughters are together for all eternity.
I declare today that you shall see,
We all shall be set free!

I am that Jesus Jew, Messiah
I am that Joseph, Joshua, Jeshua;
As Adam, I lost the Kingdom (of my life)
But gained it back later through Christ,

(With Him) DIRECTS THIS CURRENT RESURRECTION.
The judgment seat is now in session.
The world enters a wondrous birth
And only "Jews" will walk the earth.
And no more tears for Rachel, or the righteous.
Come forward, do what you can do (in love &)
Be that Jew like you!

25. Declaration of The United People of The United States of America

We hold these truths to be self-evident: That God is the 1st reality. And He has ultimate control over all events and over all circumstances. And that there is, in truth, only One God, though He may be called by many names.

And that God created man in His image. And man is, as it were, a spark of God, having free will and a certain freedom of thought and action, manifesting throughout the universe for maintenance, growth, and development. And that God created all that there is. And everything that He has created has a time and it has a season.

And that some of God's creation has been in rebellion against God and they have been at war with man for times and seasons, for thousands of years. And you can tell who they are by what they do, and you can tell who they are by what they say- because they do wrong and they tell lies, and they are Oppressors, and tyrants, and devils.

And that their time has come to an end. And their season must make way for Our Season. And it is Our time, now!

For, with all due respect to Mr. Jefferson, this truth is self-evident: government of the people, by the people, and for the people has been tried, and it has failed.

And the failure was for many reasons. But foremost, it failed because the 1st reality was made secondary, tertiary, a footnote, an afterthought, or omission.

And during the time of the birth of the nation, though talk of liberty came out of many mouths- when we WATCH the hands, we see them grabbing at freedom for self, but choosing chains for others.

And so, a great civil war was fought, and the war was fought among brothers and relatives, kinsmen, and neighbors. And the war did not turn until there was a decision to choose what was right, and until there was a realization that the belief that right makes might must be an applied principle, and not just a saying.

And though Mr. Lincoln may have desired such, there really was no sustained rebirth of freedom. The rebirth was in many ways as bad as the birth. It was halfhearted. It was hypocritical. It had no substance. Some effort, by some, lasted a few years. Then, it fizzled. And the counter attack by the tyrants and Oppressors prevailed.

And within 10-years, justice was lifeless and stillborn, the nation grew in hypocrisy in real life, and the pursuit of happiness rang hollow because the nation was not true to itself, because it was still living in de facto denial, exclusion, Oppression, and evil. For, the ideal was only stated, it was not applied.

But we come not to transcend Mr. Jefferson or Mr. Lincoln, but we come to honor them, and to further enshrine them, because they are great men. And we recognize them for their efforts, and we look to them as our mentors in many ways. And we believe that they are worthy to be honored and emulated.

But, there was no freedom after the war fought against tyranny. And there was no freedom after the war fought over slavery. And the hope for a REBIRTH of freedom died along with the birth of Jim Crow.

So, 100-years later, there was a great Civil Rights Movement, and that was supposed to be yet another rebirth of freedom. And though due process has progressed to embrace and emancipate women, and the disabled- exclusion, denial, and Oppression are still rampant.

And they pass laws on top of laws. And they add amendments to amendments. And the country, and the world becomes more enslaved. And society becomes more dysfunctional because the values and forms are defective, and that is so because the distortions were instituted by that same Prince that Mr. Jefferson so eloquently demanded separation from.

And, as I said, Mr. Jefferson is our mentor, and he is right:
IT IS OUR RIGHT! IT IS OUR DUTY TO THROW OFF this present intrusive, parasitic, ineffective, and oppressive government by those princes in rebellion against God!

And we shall institute a form of government of God and people, for God and people, for the Glory of God!

And Our government shall be an Everlasting Government that shall not depart from what is right, and it will not stray from justice, nor deny dignity and sufficient substance to any of its citizens.

And those in rebellion against God and at war with man will be thrown off the face of the earth, just as they were ousted from Heaven.

So, today, we must separate ourselves from the values, and policies, and ideas of those who say evil things, and do what is wrong. This is what they do:

1- They limit supplies to artificially prop up prices;

2- They create unemployment to increase the labor pool to keep down wages;

3- They maintain a low minimum wage to create extensive and maximum misery;

4- They waste good food, clothing, and other products to maintain high prices;

5- They call our children kids; and they teach them by example, selfishness, and materialism; and to behave like lower animals;

6- They call a certain cake, "devil's food cake," and then they eat it.

7- They call a people having a rainbow of colors, "black;"

8- Their involvement in Bosnia shows that they are cowards; and they have no awareness that "right makes might;"

9- They warehouse people in prisons and the minimum number of workers will support them because of employment practices;

10- And they warehouse prisoners to create employment;

11- And the prisons they create are a cesspool of iniquity;

12- Their concept of government is that government is a parasite and leech off the people; and this is what they practice;

13- They have been known to call thorough mis-education (because many of the foundations are either wrong or faulty), higher education;

14- They make formal education too much of a production race, like Chicago rush hour traffic down Michigan Avenue; but Jefferson and Lincoln (who had only about 1 year of formal education) are examples of the educated; and real education is more like taking a Sunday drive, zooming down I57; or even taking a leisurely stroll;

15- They over price just about everything; and they value things of limited worth;

16- They perpetuate a pervasive system that advances inferiority in nature, character, and morality through medical practice, education, and social policy; they have been known to implant lower animal parts in human beings; they promote an excessive use of drugs; and they don't seem to realize that morality is based on justice, caring, and sharing, and that proper character is the application of those values in DAILY living;

17- They generally train people, in the educational system, to be commodity-cogs in the production system, and to be tools to exploit, manipulate, and monopolize markets and resources;

18- They all too often make the work place and work undesirable endeavors, though they should be opportunities for providing service (caring and sharing); creating, like Our Father (production); time for self-discovery and personal growth; and to realize that all work is honorable, if you are an honorable person;

19- They exclude people from participation in society, put them on welfare; and then they exploit, oppress, and tyrannize them;

20- They failed to provide compensation (or land), and rehabilitation services for the millions held in captivity for decades, but did so for the 53 held in captivity for 444 days by Iran;

21- They wage physical, psychological, and economic warfare against many of the citizens through police brutality and oppression, negative reporting (and stereotyping), systemic discriminations in employment, housing, education, etc., and denial of credit;

22- They create wholly unnecessary homelessness and other ills through irrational economic and social policy;

23- They create conditions to create crime, to create police to create employment;

24- They allow drugs into the society to keep the people drugged up so they won't be sober enough to fight their Oppressors;

25- They maintain a so-called free press (news media) to titillate, amuse, and distract the people away from the activities of the REAL PLAYERS- the money supply manipulators (the Federal Reserve System), business, and the slavish government, which obediently does the bidding of business;

26- They maintain a constant barrage of "sports" activities to distract the people;

27- Their media programming and other productions are often demeaning of God's creation, blasphemous, and unfit for human consumption;

28- They created an anti-intellectual, pro-ignorance, "pro-clown," pro-athletics climate in many communities, and whenever enlightenment and liberation appeared, it faced opposition and oppression;

29- They divided Americans along tribal lines and taught them to see themselves as black-white, Native American, Hispanic, gay, and in other balkanized ways-for easier control and manipulation by the oppressors;

30- They have given business intrusive, tyrannical, and despotic powers over the people; and the business crimes AGAINST THE PEOPLE of theft, fraud, lying, perjury, deception, and other injustices are responded to by a slap on the wrist (if anything);

31- They tell workers to be more and more productive; and their jobs become less and less secure;

32- Rather than technology and automation being a liberating agent, the record is spotty; they are used to enslave here, to entrench those in power there; they are used to create unemployment also, and contribute to homelessness; and they are used to do the wrong things;

33- They have made government administrations intrusive, weak, wasteful, impotent, unresponsive, yet destructive;

34- They created a huge $15 trillion debt because they have a small thinking capacity;

35- They have tried to make the abominable practice of homosexuality respectable;

36- They have intruded themselves into the sanctity of the bedroom and marriage relationships of the people, and their mere presence there would tend to defile those sacred relationships because such intrusions are unnatural;

37- They have made prostitution "legal" in some places; and their crimes against our mothers, sisters, and daughters are high crimes against nature;

38- They engage various levels of government in gambling, in the areas that include lottery, horses, and casinos;

39- They gave undue financial rewards and set bad examples of dirty mouth devils, especially so-called comedians, for polluting the country and people with low class language, ideas, and ways of expression;

40- And they have failed to reward and promote good Americans who know and respect the language, laws, customs, and traditions of our righteous ancestors; but instead they promote the ignorant, slavish, tyrannical types who do the unjust bidding of the devils;

41- Their religious messages are NOT strong on justice, mercy, forgiveness, rehabilitation, and redemption; rather they are filled with mealy-mouthed platitudes that often rationalize or overlook the systemic sickness of the society; and some of it is an unnecessary and misplaced guilt trip about "sexuality" and "original sin;" and they don't sufficiently recognize the divinity and goodness in all of God's creation;

42- They TRAFFIC IN CHILDREN through agencies that barter away children into foster care, other substitute care, and adoption, for pay checks, stipends, and other benefits- sometimes illegally and fraudulently stealing children from good and deserving (grieving) mothers and fathers; and because of the irrational economics of the society, the working segment of the populace pays for these transactions;

43- They created an intolerable worldwide system of exploitation, and subjugation of peoples based on their ignorant and intolerant social views, irrational economic system, and injustice, despotism, and tyranny; so WWI was nature's response, by beginning to dismantle and dislodge them from the earth; and in WWII, Korea, and Viet Nam, God held up the MIRRORS of Nazism, Fascism, and Communism (Materialism); and the wars were not concluded until decisions and choices were made to try to do what is right;

and He allowed them to destroy some of the MIRRORS, and to realize that you don't necessarily have to win a military war to be a winner, BUT THEY STILL JUST DON'T GET IT!

44- They balkanized many parts of the world and sowed the seeds for future conflicts by arbitrarily dividing nations (and tribes) of peoples in Africa, Europe, Asia, etc.;

45- They made the USA part of the 7th World Power (Empire, consisting of the USA, Canada, the U.K., and Australia), and also part of the 8th (and last) World Power that includes the 7th Power, plus the European Union, NATO, et. al.; and the inclination of these powers is generally to do what is evil, or expedient first, and not what is right;

46- They created the State of Israel, even though THESE UNITED STATES OF AMERICA IS MORE ANALOGOUS, EVEN SYNONYMOUS WITH ANCIENT ISRAEL THAN THAT COLONIAL STATE CALLED ISRAEL, BOTH IN ITS GOODNESS (UNIQUENESS), AND IN ITS EVIL; But "Israel," in its true meaning is NOT confined to the USA, et. al. borders, but rather, includes those who join in the Tradition and Mission as put forth through the previous and current prophets;

47- They have created a so-called third world, and developing world of misery through local incompetents (puppets), neocolonialism, irrational economic policy, the IMF, and the World Bank;

And for 219 years this Prince has come to the American people throughout the year, and especially every 2 years, at election time; and every 4 years, at election time.

And the Prince has come with a plan to build more prisons, and more prisons, for more and more prisoners. And the Prince does not tell you that when you put those people in prisons, THEN YOU MUST SUPPORT THEM, because prisoners are not allowed to work and to be "self-supporting."

And the Prince does not tell you that if the society was not so dysfunctional, and irrational, there would be little, or no need for the prisons. And the Prince does not tell you that THIS SOCIETY IS HARDLY CAPABLE OF REHABILITATION because of inherent knowledge deficiency; and also, rehabilitation is not a priority or objective of THE SYSTEM.

And these Princes come with plans to extend an unwarrantable jurisdiction over the people in the areas of health insurance, and other areas because business IS TOO PRINCELY TO DO IT; and the Princes want to control God's creation; and they want to create a job for themselves.

And they tell workers to be more productive and more efficient. But the more efficient the workers have become, the more they become expendable because they build up inventory more quickly. And with the fast inventory buildup capability, the employer doesn't need to employ the current employee, plus another guy. But the other guy still needs sustenance, so the worker works more hours to support him (in jail, or on welfare).

And the schools, also, become less true to their mission, because they don't tell the truth about the society, and the need for fundamental change. Rather, they promote the lies! And metal detectors are installed in some schools because the truth will eventually catch up to the lies!

So, this is the time for good people to catch those princes of injustice and duplicity and bind them for 1000 years. First, We will get them to identify themselves by their choosing to oppose "Jubilee," bartering, AND OTHER RIGHTEOUS measures handed down through Our God and His servant, Moses.

And then He will take them, and show you that these "princes" are no princes at all, but rather, low forms of life, and fit fuel for hell fire.

So, We here today declare that from henceforth, and forevermore, good people are, and of right, ought to be, separate, and apart from Oppressors, tyrants, and devils. And, that the good will move into and within their choice of right values, cultures, and institutions. And that the devils will go to the place where they belong!

And the earth will become the home of God's dear chosen! And truth and justice will become a way of life.

WE'LL HOLD THESE TRUTHS AS EVIDENCE: For, we will truly walk in freedom. And tell the truth. And prophesy, philosophy. And dream. And build myriad, boundless monuments to Him. And listen as our children sing. And the earth will ring with the joyous sounds of those who made the choice of caring, sharing; unity of self, and with Our Father; and knowledge will MULTIPLY and flower like abundant springtime.

And We will sing this:

FREE AT LAST

FREE AT LAST

THANK GOD ALMIGHTY

WE'RE FREE AT LAST!

26. SHE IS THE TEMPLE OF THE LIVING GOD

She is the Temple of The Living God
An apparel, adornment for him
So, go ahead, adore and love her
Sharing all you have.

And he is The Temple of The Living God
An apparel, adornment for her
So, share your all with him.

Then, fight for love, in the world:

Go, love a Mormon, Muslim, Jew, Hindu, Sikh, Buddhist, Adventist, "Witness."

Love an American today. Then, love an Asian, an African, a European.

Go, love a Native American. And don't stop there.

Even, love an atheist, materialist, the selfish (they need a lot of love).

Then, wage a Holy War Of Love:

Of caring, sharing,
And daring Adorations.

Adopt The Declaration of Love

Complete Our Spiritual Revolution
And overthrow the evil devils.

Get Independent
Adore the Origin of Love (inside, outside)
He resides in everyone, (and out there).

Then, get eternal, universal citizenship
And care, and share
With daring adorations
Of The Temple of God.

27. FREE AT LAST

Gabriel blew His horn
And countless angels came here,
Marched against the devils,
To the beat of God

And Babylon, the Great
Came in remembrance before God
To be judged for its abominations and oppressions
And the USA became financially bankrupt
With a $15 trillion debt
Because its economics are out of step with God

And it became morally, intellectually, and politically bankrupt.
Hurricanes came up; tornadoes tore;
And earthquakes rumbled against the devils
Because its nature is out of step with God.

Joshua marched with Gabriel,
And the walls came tumbling down!
Because the foundation is faulty and evil.

And One Million Men joined Joshua, Gabriel, and God
To bury Babylon
For, the righteous began to mobilize to replace
What is out of step with God.

They marched: <u>One,</u> for Unity with self and God
(And we will have this Spiritual Revolution that leads to Unity,
With our Atonement, reconciliation, and responsibility)

<u>Two</u> is for the 2nd Coming of Caring and Sharing
(For We will share the bounty of the earth, and there will truly be justice for all)

<u>Three</u> is for nation building and rebirth;
For the nation will be reborn, to last forever

And <u>four</u>, God will defeat and bind the devils for
A thousand years!

And all those who remain on earth will march in step with
Joshua, Gabriel, and God:

  All together
  Keeping the beat!

  And you will see
  A symphony of beauty,
  Singing:

FREE AT LAST!
FREE AT LAST!
THANK GOD ALMIGHTY,
WE'RE FREE AT LAST!"

28 ABOUT THE AUTHOR, AND OTHER BOOKS

Youssef Khalim obtained Unity in yoga on about 7/20/80. He says, "We will recombine into one faith, Judaism, Christianity, and Islam." He has been able to "see" and experience some amazing information about USA presidents Jefferson, Lincoln, and Obama; and also Prophets Moses, Muhammad, and Solomon - in visions, lucid dreams, and in meditation. Khalim makes reincarnation (resurrection) central again in our western religions. He resides in the Chicagoland area. And he is the father of Tonya, Runako, and Noah. See his books on the following websites: http://lulu.com and http://sunracommunications.com

Other Books

Youssef Khalim's books include *People Of The Future/Day; You Are Too Beautiful; I Love You Back; The Resurrection Of Noah; Jubilee Worldwide; Lara, Forever; Tanisha Love; Galina, All About Love; I Call My Sugar, Candie; Natalia, With Love; Svetlana, Angel Of Love; Lori, My Dream Girl; Love of My Life*; and *The Second Coming!*

www.ingramcontent.com/pod-product-compliance
Lightning Source LLC
Chambersburg PA
CBHW032135090426
42743CB00007B/609